WINGLESS

poems by

Zachary Riddle

Finishing Line Press
Georgetown, Kentucky

WINGLESS

in memory of my father, Michael Allen Riddle
(February 1st, 1955—October 11th, 2013)

Copyright © 2018 by Zachary Riddle
ISBN 978-1-63534-535-3 First Edition
All rights reserved under International and Pan-American Copyright Conventions.
No part of this book may be reproduced in any manner whatsoever without written permission from the publisher, except in the case of brief quotations embodied in critical articles and reviews.

ACKNOWLEDGMENTS

Literary Magazines & Journals

Apex: — Wingless

The Ghazal Page: — Do Not Resuscitate

Glassworks Magazine: — Homecoming

Icarus Down Review: — Aquaphobia

Into the Void: — The Only Oblivion

Open Palm Print: — After the Dark
The First Time I Killed You

Temenos: — Revelations After Watching Nosferatu

The Voidwalker Review: — October Requiem

Chapbooks

This Labyrinth We Wander — A Son Remembers His Father
The Last Elegy for My Father

Competitions and Prizes

Poetry Jett/National Poetry Month Prize—March 2015 — Wingless

Publisher: Leah Maines
Editor: Christen Kincaid
Cover Art: Amanda Shepard
Author Photo: Zachary Riddle
Cover Design: Elizabeth Maines McCleavy

Printed in the USA on acid-free paper.
Order online: www.finishinglinepress.com
also available on amazon.com

Author inquiries and mail orders:
Finishing Line Press
P. O. Box 1626
Georgetown, Kentucky 40324
U. S. A.

Table of Contents

Buried in the Dark 1
Wingless 2
Apocalypse 4
Phantom Pain 5
Revelations After Watching *Nosferatu* 6
May Requiem 8
June Requiem 9
July Requiem 10
The First Time I Killed You 11
Aquaphobia 12
August Requiem 14
September Requiem 15
Revelations After Watching *The Haunting* 16
Homecoming 17
The Sixth Dream 19
October Requiem 20
Revelations After Watching *The Blair Witch Project* 21
November Requiem 22
February Requiem 23
Light Keeper 24
April Requiem 25
A Son Remembers His Father 26
2013 27
Do Not Resuscitate 28
The Only Oblivion 29
After the Dark 31
The Last Elegy for My Father 32

...how is it that this lives in thy mind?
—William Shakespeare
   The Tempest

You see it too? For me, it's always like this.
—Hiroyuki Owaku & Takayoshi Sato
   Silent Hill 2

Buried in the Dark

As a child, the first corpse I saw was sprawled
beneath a tree with candles on the tips

of its leafless branches: a little girl,
her lips bruised blue, her irises empty,

cheekbones broken, hands bound
behind her back. When my mother

walked into the living room and saw
the body

on the television, she sent me
to bed without supper, told me I knew

I wasn't supposed to watch
shows like that. Later, I asked her what

happened when we died. She told me,
Every woman is cursed by the man buried

inside of her. I never even wanted
kids. Not really. Our step-dad watched us

from the living room window. Mom jabbed
her trowel into the garden dirt

as my brother and I baked
in the front lawn.

Wingless

i.

Wings burst from my back when I was ten
years old. It was genetic, passed down through

my father's heritage. Thick, dark feathers grew
from my shoulders.

My classmates pointed. My teacher told me
I was mythology, said I needed a doctor.

My brother called me *Crow*, asked me when we'd
fly together. My mother, redeyed, wrapped

my head in cloth, bound my hands and ankles
with duct tape, dragged me to the front yard, and took

        a gutknife to my newborn
        flesh and feather.

ii.

My brother's body sank into an ice bath,
his sunburned skin beet-red, his round eyes

pinched shut. Grandma ran a cardboard
colored washcloth across

his forehead and twisted
it tightly around his neck. The blisters

on his shoulders seeped thick
yellow that pooled on the water's

surface. She kneeled by the tub
and from between the half-closed curtains

a blot of sunset made haven
on her forearm. When he healed,

    we compared the scars on our backs.
    His: pale and glossed, and mine: rigid and stitched.

Apocalypse

My father's body was covered in black stars.
He used to tell us stories about God

and the end days. They were always the same:
an asteroid struck the moon, split it in two,

and the oceans swallowed shorelines, trees, cities.
The first moon, he said, *is bright as the sun.*

The second moon is blue, but smaller.
Both share the horizon like brothers

from the same broken womb.
When we asked if we would die,

he wrapped us in his wings,
kept us warm, whispered into the black

of the room: *A great metal dragon will emerge*
from the deep earth, iris carved from iron,

guts built from gears. The world will plunge into chaos.
That's how the stories always ended.

He left us not long after. My brother and I felt forests growing
inside our chests, our stomachs stirring with soil and ash.

Phantom Pain

As I grew older, I starting dreaming more,
started seeing things that weren't really there.

The first corpse appeared in the driveway.
I sat next to it, ran my hands

through its thin, blonde hair, pulled back its blue
bottom lip to unveil yellowing teeth.

I decided it was a woman, so I painted
the corpse's face with my mother's makeup.

The corpse and I spent most of the winter together.
We played dress-up, built snow forts and snowmen

and caught snowflakes on our tongues. One night,
after my mother came home from the factory,

she saw specks of mascara on my hand,
lipstick on my wrist, and told me

boys weren't to play with their mother's things.
I tried to show her the woman,

tried to explain how I unkilled her.
My mother refused to see the body I wanted

her to see. The next morning,
I couldn't see her either.

Revelations After Watching *Nosferatu*

Act I

As a boy, I was obsessed with transformation.
    My grandmother was the first to know I hated the idea of my body.
    She sat me on my grandfather's lap. He was made of dark—I was
    made of crowfeathers.

One night, I saw his shadow, thinboned and fanged,
    crawl into the kitchen. He opened his mouth and swallowed
    moonlight as it poured through the window. I think he knew I
    was watching.

Act II

I hadn't seen a blackandwhite film until I was older:
    I watched as the door creaked open and the ratfaced,
    crackednailed phantom hovered
    into the guest bedroom. *Why do you watch this shit?*
    my mother asked.

I gestured to the fractures
    in her forehead, to the bodies sewn into the walls. My brother sat
    silent on the floor, crosslegged and gapemouthed, staring at the
    television.

Act III

On his deathbed, I told my father I was the last of his line—
    that I lived in a self-discovered cataclysm—
    that I couldn't promise him grandchildren because I wouldn't be
    able to bear them.

I told him he wasn't forgiven,
    that God had devoured much smaller bodies than his. The nurse
    explained his wings were lost in surgery. She handed me a jar of
    ash and smiled.

Act IV

After the funeral, my brother cried like a newborn.
    I said, *The casket felt weightless.*
    He shouted, *You're always going on and on about being haunted.*

I left after the viewing.
    Between the stars, burning locusts—on the side of the highway,
    an emaciated wolf gnawing at the brittle bones of a deer.

Act V

It wasn't long before I started staring
    aimlessly into bodies of water. I dreamt I saw a girl's face, pale
    and emaciated,
    pressed against the side of a bathtub. I wrapped my hands around
    her skull, pushed my thumbs to her temples. I strained to save her.

May Requiem

I was sitting on the couch when the house phone
rang. *It's been a while, son*, you said.

You asked me how I'd been. I refused, at first,
to believe it was you. The you I remembered

ate bowlfuls of chili at a run-down restaurant
in the old part of town. The you I remembered

rode a worn lawn mower at four in the morning
through knee high weeds. The you I remembered

told me not to be afraid while
The Texas Chainsaw Massacre buzzed

in the background of your makeshift bedroom
in your friend's country home. You held me tight,

my seven-year-old face pressed into your flannel.
There's nothing to be scared of, you said.

It isn't real.
But all I heard were screams.

June Requiem

You sat next to me at the picnic table outside your mother's motor home, our white shirts and torn jeans sweatsoaked in the summer heat.

I never knew I mirrored you—bulged veins on the backs of our hands, thinhaired, slimfaced. You put a cigarette between your lips,

told me you were glad I never smoked, that my mother did right by me all these years. Your jaw was slanted, most of your teeth

missing or yellowed. You were thinner than I remembered, thinner than I was. When you tried to apologize for your ten-year absence,

you told me that your brother had been cooking meth and the FBI was searching for him and you didn't want us caught up

the way you were caught up all your life. You told me I shouldn't drink because your father drank, and his father drank,

and one night your father drank so much he handed you a shotgun and told you to shoot him if you hated him so much.

You told me dinner would be ready soon. Told me you'd always be my father. That you didn't know you were dying.

July Requiem

When I arrived at the hospital, my half-
sister asked me if we should unplug you.
We walked into the ICU, the two of us

and the nurse. A patient in one of the rooms
screamed *God, God, God* at the top of his lungs,
over and over. I recalled the only memory

I had of you in the snow:
you hoisted me onto your plaid jacket
shoulders and carried me outside.

We couldn't see the street underneath the white.
Cars on the highway barked in the distance.
You put me down, and I sank to my waist

while you laid out and spread your arms and legs.
It's an angel, you said. I sloshed through the snow
and sat small in the outline of your body.

*He'd be strapped to an IV for the rest
of his life*, the nurse said.
A red-edged moth, dead in the windowsill.

The First Time I Killed You

I asked my brother if he would come with me
to unplug you, and he told me he didn't want to,

that the man on a ventilator in downtown Kalamazoo wasn't
his father. Your body anchored like a motorboat for the long winter ahead.

I remember, as boys, I'd ghostcall to get my mother's attention, say *Joshua!*
Joshua! Dad is here! And my brother, longing for your fatherly touch

on the curve of his cheek, streaked toward the backdoor, smilescreaming.
The driveway was empty. My mother slapped me.

I think I knew I killed you, then, too.

Aquaphobia

       i.

My father taught me to cast
fishing line into fishless
ponds. The bob sat stagnant
on a film of algae and feathers
and trash. He left my brother
and me alone on the dock
in the spring heat,
my reflection in the shadow
of a budding tree. I wished
I was with my mother.
                      We never caught a thing.

      ii.

I held my father's hand tight in mine
the week before he died. His blue
eyes shimmered. I imagined
a vast lake. On the shore, the house
he promised my brother and me
years ago. *I'll get a nice one, boys,*
he said. *You'll see.*
I promise.
                      I promised, too.

      iii.

I try to swim, but I fear
the cool splash on my neck,
the back of my ears. All I want
is to breathe. You told me, once,
not to take the water into
my lungs, but it's what my mother
taught me to do when my body
sunk wave after wave, my feet
shivering, toes digging

into the silt on the lake's bottom.
I have no choice.

August Requiem

The pastor told us you wanted to leave
more for me. Your mother,

who I had only met three times before,
folded my hand in hers. Your casket

was surrounded by daffodils.
I wanted to stand, apologize for being

your son, haul your body to my car
and drive two hours to my apartment

and wash you from the hair on your head
to the soles of your feet.

I wanted to lock the bathroom,
leave you in the water until your body

rotted and filled with maggots. I wanted
to bring you supper every night and spoon

oatmeal and chopped sausage and cherries
into your grayed mouth. After you were buried,

everyone asked me why I'd been gone so long,
why I hadn't called for ten years, why my hands

were shaking. I waited to sob until
I was on the highway.

September Requiem

The morning after your funeral,
a blood matted wolf with great, black wings

stood in the doorway of her apartment.
The wolf stepped into the kitchen

and rested its head on my lap.
She asked me if I'd slept well.

I thought for a moment about the missed
phone calls, about her growing collection

of peach vodka bottles and beer cans,
about the chimera that crawled between us

in the night, its snake tail wound around my legs,
its lion teeth tense against my throat.

The wolf nudged my elbow with its nose.
It reminded me of you. I didn't know what to say.

Revelations After Watching *The Haunting*

I was born haunted.
I listened to my childhood
home churn, my mother's house.
I begged for nothing to come
crawling out of the dark
separating my brother's room
from my own. I often imagined all
the ways the house would swallow me.
On weekends, our father took us.
We'd sit silently on the couch, half-eaten
lasagna cooling on the sticky
poker table. Photographs of Elvis
lined the walls. The carpet covered
with dirt and fur and beer. *I want
to have you out here more often,*
he said, *if your mom's okay with it.*
The trailer home tightened around us
like a swollen throat. Family members
I'd never met stared, statues molded
from the mud beneath the dead
lawn. It always rained
when we visited. That night
I sweat-slept on the stained
mattress of a foldout futon.
I'd never felt so small.

Homecoming

i.

When I visited my hometown for the first time in six months, it had become a gigantic funeral home. Instead of streets, there were hallways and offices and makeshift morgues. All of the residents worked for the funeral home, preparing corpses that had been sent from other cities across the state for viewings, funerals, and burials. I walked to the outskirts of Funeral Home City to visit my father's grave, but there was no cemetery. Instead, I found a man who claimed to be the world's last horseback rider. He was sitting on a saddled pile of horse bones next to a forest filled with dead trees. He told me the forest was for bodies that weren't fit for funerals, left for the animals and the poor to eat. He said he had visions of this world, swallowed by oceans he'd never seen, two-mooned and dark. *Probably, that's how it'll end*, he said. I asked if I would be arrested if I dug for my father's body, and he shook his head. *You've been here before. You always end up here.*

ii.

The house where I grew up was sectioned off from Funeral Home City with caution tape. I looked through my old bedroom window. The inside of the house had flooded. All of the light bulbs were burnt out. Bills and unopened letters floated on the water's surface. My mother sat on my bed. I knocked on the window, and she looked at me with eyes like planets in the night sky. I asked her if I could come in, and she started to take off her clothes. She stood in the waist deep water, pressed her breasts against the window, eyes red-veined. In the backyard, the gazebo had fallen apart, the shed rotted, my brother's punching bag covered in blood. There were nine empty graves. My stepfather laid on the patio, covered in dirt. He wiped the sweat from his brow and asked me why I had come home, and I told him I wanted to be lost again. He rolled his eyes and talked about the weather. *I'm going to grow a forest once it rains*, he said, *just like your mother always wanted*. He started to cry, and for the first time, I saw the stretch-scars on the underside of his gut, on the soles of his feet, the palms of his hands. *All men become their fathers*, he told me iii.

I found my brother in his truck next to the doughnut shop, which had also become a part-time coffin contracting office. He didn't hear me at first, but when I sat in the passenger seat, he looked at me with teary eyes and asked me why I'd been gone so long. I wrapped my arms around him, and we watched the drunks file out of the bar across the street. After a while, he started his truck. He told me he knew what it was I was looking for. While he drove, neither of us spoke. My brother pulled into the driveway of an old motor home in the borderlands of Funeral Home City. I stepped out of the truck, surrounded by chest-high weeds. He pointed ahead, told me: *I won't see you again, you know, not until you've lost everything. I won't know that I know you.* After his car was swallowed by backroad, I entered the motor home and stood at the grease-stained countertop in the kitchen. My grandmother's corpse was face down in a pile of unwashed dishes.

iv.

I cut open my grandmother's body and stepped into her one leg at a time, each foot grounding on soft, grassless soil. I was surrounded by tombstones and billowing trees. A plague doctor greeted me, offered to guide me through this world and lead me to my father's grave. He told me the story of each of the men and women buried around us: *This is Funeral Home City's Cemetery for the Lost,* he said. The plague doctor whispered: *Only three sets of eyes have graced this sanctuary.* I asked him if we could talk about something else, and he laughed, *Nyctohylophobia is the fear of forests at night. Did you know that?* We walked for hours. At the edge of Funeral Home City's Cemetery for the Lost, we found an abandoned cabin. Inside, the skull of a crow sitting atop a cracked pedestal, a birthday card wedged in its beak. I leaned against the pedestal and slid to the floor with the card in my hands. It was soaked through with water, the cartoon balloons on the front wrinkled, the purple ink smudged: *I've never hurt anything that wasn't worth hurting.* My own name was signed at the bottom. The Plague Doctor admitted to that he'd led many versions of me down this same path before. He says, *You are proof of your father's deadness.*

The Sixth Dream

I spend the first quarter of the dream killing you all over again.

Your left arm is hairless and pale, nails cracked and dirty.

Your right arm is tanned and freckled, an IV jutting from moon blue veins.

My hands are covered in your gore.

I'm standing beneath the sick hospital lights.

The part of your family that loves the left half of your body is speechless.

The part of your family that loves the right half of your body is sobbing.

My baby boy, your mother says, cradling your head in her arms.

Later, I am sitting in a dingy bathroom in the only stall that has a lock.

The toilet seat is loose and uncomfortable.

The fluorescent lights flicker on and off, on and off, on and off.

You and I are the same.

The murdered and the monsters.

A twisted face with crooked teeth.

October Requiem

When I went looking for you after you died,
all I found was the worn gravestone

of the first woman you loved and the child
who died in her arms, my infant half-brother.

I wish I'd known you before your body
was lost beneath an unmarked patch

of yellowed grass, before I told myself
that I wouldn't become your absence.

Every bone in my body is shaped as yours,
every hair that stands on the back of my neck,

the way I slip beneath the water's surface,
the way I learned to drown.

I want to pinch this cemetery small
between my fingers, tuck it beneath

my tongue so you can feel my words
as they slide between my lips,

every breath an infinite conversation
between our bodies, father and son.

Revelations After Watching *The Blair Witch Project*

        My father taught my brother and me

to hunt mushrooms in the brush   behind the city's twin cemeteries

taught us how to fetch kindling

                      how to cast flame

    how to strike up a tent

        to sleep on the hill overlooking

    his mother's tin can

        trailer home.

      We spend our lives

        wandering

        in violent

          circles.

              The first ghost

                      story I learn to tell:

    it is impossible

to outrun the bodies

            that haunt us.

November Requiem

I am trying to watch *The Fly*, but you keep telling me the same story, over and over, about all of the farm animals you and your father and grandfather stole. *There was this one time, we rode up to this guy's farm. Didn't think he was home,* you said, *and dad told me, get your ass over that fence and snag the whole goddamn coop.* You pause and wait for me to ask what happened, but I don't. You say: *When I came back with the coop, dad and granddad were gone. There was just a scarecrow and the moon and the owner of the barn, flashlight in one hand, shotgun in the other. He beat me. Spat on me before he left me on the side of the road.* On screen, Jeff Goldblum is not Jeff Goldblum, but a man-fly-machine crawling toward the woman he once loved. And you are not you. You are a wolf sitting on a futon two months after your funeral, lapping at the spilled rice on the floor.

February Requiem

You spend most of your time lying
in front of my door, now, your head

rested between your front legs.
Whenever I move, you open your black

eyes and track me, stand and growl
until I am curled tight in the corner of my bed.

You urinate on my clothes, chew holes in the carpet,
bring me dead squirrels and possums and raccoons.

You drag a stag onto my lap, its tongue spilling
from its open mouth. *Prove you are alive*, you say.

I take the stag by its antlers, slit its throat, smear blood
on my face. I carve a wolf mask from the birch trees

behind my home. You lead me down a thin path
to a clearing. We stand, my bare feet

and your padded paws soft on crushed queen's
lace, our noses pointed toward the ashen sky.

Light Keeper

From the grave, you remind me
there is nothing in this world

but the violent dark.
My hands will always be

stained with you. You lurk
in evening closet shadows cast

by clothes that I've since outgrown,
a forest where pieces of you hang

from dead branches, your blood thick
between the fading constellations,

intestines wrapped around Hercules'
shoulders. Every night, I carve cities

out of my body to make space for the ruins
of your ghost: I am your possessed,

your empty hallway,
the lighthouse overlooking

the sea of ways
I will become you.

April Requiem

You wrap me in your carrion wings the way you did when I was a child. We're in the field outside your mother's trailer. A breeze rustles the whiskers on your snout. You close your eyes, whisper my name, remind me that I'll always be a killer. I grab your jaw with my hands. You crush my fingers between your teeth. My back arcs against soil. *You don't have to wait much longer,* you say. I plummet a knife into your chest and two shredded leather wings burst from my back, dripping with blood and pus and mud. I scream my mother's freckled face, scream the years I believed I wasn't me, scream your motionless body writhing on a hospital bed. When I am covered in our blood—yours, and mine—I remember what it means to be alive. I remember what it means to be your son.

A Son Remembers His Father

This is what you refuse to know: you can't unkill your father. You've murdered him one thousand times in the same papier-mâché hospital. You keep waiting for the world to fold in on itself, to make a clear path to a lighthouse on the east coast, far away from your home, but you know that isn't how it works. Things don't just fold and unfold. Your mouth, a shell. No one, not even the ocean, can open you, convince you to spit out the marble of light you harbor beneath your tongue.

2013

after Zachary Schomburg

i.

I was born a funeral flower. Everyone wants me to smile during my Dad's viewing, to pretend it's okay, but I can't, and it isn't, because I didn't choose to live the last moments of my life in a plaster vase, my feet submerged in chilled water, waiting to be tossed on the casket's mahogany top. I will be covered in dirt by two men who bring home weekly two-hundred dollar paychecks to a starved wife and three children. I will not regrow. I will die a funeral flower. I will die a funeral flower. I will die. I will

ii.

Do Not Resuscitate

When I was a boy, you and I went fishing, Dad.
Over the phone I said *Let's go! I'm itching*, Dad.

You picked me up at grandma's house. Mom was sleeping
upstairs. She couldn't stand to see your bound wings, Dad.

I slid my hook through the knotted body of a worm,
felt the soft earth burst from its gut living, Dad.

The first fish I caught dangled at the end of my pole.
It flopped in the air, twisting, Dad.

I watched as you plucked it, firm in your tunnel hands,
held its scaled face to yours. You were listening, Dad,

as it told a story about life underwater,
but you dropped it in a bucket unforgiving, Dad.

And that's all I remember, now: not the car ride home,
not the summer heat. I remember the wriggling, the writhing, Dad.

I remember your body, tangled in tubes and wires,
your eyes caked shut from hours of sleeping, Dad.

When the nurse woke you, I remember your lips
chapped, begging for words. Begging, Dad.

I remember the fish swirling in its dingy white prison. I wondered
if it knew what it was like to be almost-*not there*, diminishing, Dad,

and for two years, I've carried your ghost in a bucket filled with
bluegill and boiling water, because I can't stop remembering, Dad,

the empty three-hour drive only to tell my family I'd be the one holding
    you—
me, your second son—unplugging you, killing you, Dad.

The Only Oblivion

I've wasted so much time
twisting our truth
like hair around a finger—
the man I've become isn't
the man I chose
to be. I'm wingless.

Dad, your black-feathered wings
once stretched wide every time
you held me. After you died, I chose
to be more than your absent truth.
You wanted me to be everything I wasn't.
I drew our tragedy in finger-paint,

but mom wrapped her third-shift fingers
around my throat and slashed my wings
because I wasn't
what she needed—a timely
reminder of her first harsh truth:
I was the result of a childish choice.

An unfair choice. An empty choice.
I am my mother's frail fingers.
But this is not the truth
I've been hiding from. Wingless
means *I'll become you, in time.*
Abandoned. In pain. Nothing

hurts as bad as knowing I'm not
how anyone says anything. I chose
to want, eventually, the body that time
gave to me, but God snapped his fingers
and decided feathers and wings
weren't the truth

I deserved. The truth
was what it's always been: I didn't

want you to die, Dad. Your wings
were buried in a blue cemetery I chose
to keep beneath my tongue, a fingers-
length away. You and I were out of time.

Truly wingless. Devoured by our only oblivion,
the blood-soaked truth, the time we didn't have,
haunted by dreams of our fingers intertwined.

After the Dark

there is a barren hospital bed, the taupe linoleum tile
covered in feathers. A cracked flip phone, keys
worn, no messages. Through the window, a lake
lined with empty houses. I'm wearing a mask
the way I was taught, hiding my mythology
like a scar beneath layers of bandages and clothes.
I am surrounded by all of the corpses I have dreamt
of, their faces rotted and smeared with eyeliner
and mascara and lipstick. My father's grave
is there, beyond the lake. Prospero claimed
Caliban, said, *This thing of darkness
I acknowledge mine*. But, in the end,
I think it's the other way around.

The Last Elegy for My Father

> *"Go then. There are other worlds than these."*
> —Stephen King, *"The Dark Tower I: The Gunslinger"*

Mom told me there was no world in which you did not give your life for me, but you never gave me your life. You gave me a fishing pole and a jar of hand-picked worms, guided my fingers as I slid the hook through their wriggling bodies. You taught me the weight of your long-gone voice, still heavy on my shoulders. When I became a man, I ate food from your table, one last supper for the two of us: meatloaf, mashed potatoes, green beans, and egg noodles. It was all you could afford.

You were buried with a pack of Marlboros in the pocket of your dingy white t-shirt, five bucks in the palm of your hand for bus fare to get you where you needed to go.

You lit your way through the dark with the tip of your cigarette and a lighter. I am your last breath every morning when I take my first, your revenant, your throbbing lungs. When I kneel at your grave, I remember what your sister told me: *His spirit, it ain't done making trouble for the rest of us.* She blamed you for missing keys and runaway pets. Pranks, she said. Her eyes welled up when I told her I saw you in my dreams, but that was a lie:

> if I dreamt of you, I've now forgotten.

Zachary Riddle is the author of one co-written, self-published chapbook of poetry, titled *This Labyrinth We Wander,* available on Amazon. His poems have appeared in *Apex, The Blue Route, Glassworks Magazine,* and *Into the Void,* among several others. His first fiction piece, "The Invisible," was published by *The Hunger* in early 2018. In October 2016, he read alongside Zilka Joseph at Central Michigan University's Wellspring Literary Series. In March 2015, he was chosen as the winner of the Poetry Jett/National Poetry Month Prize, a scholarship created in 2003 by Jett Whitehead. He has acted as the Editor-in-Chief of two literary journals at CMU: *The Central Review* and *Temenos.* Zachary plans to eventually attain his M.F.A., but for the time being will continue to pursue his writing independently, working to write a screenplay, as well as finishing his longer manuscript of poetry. He thanks you for reading his work.

www.ingramcontent.com/pod-product-compliance
Lightning Source LLC
LaVergne TN
LVHW041505070426
835507LV00012B/1337